CW01390105

Datefinder

C O N T E N T S

🏭 Collins*Children'sBooks*
Copyright © HarperCollins Publishers Ltd 1996

In Ancient Times

4,600 MYA
150,000BC
24,000BC
11,000-9300BC
3500BC
3000BC

We think that life on Earth began 4,600 million years ago (MYA).

Human-like creatures (4 MYA)

Neanderthals (35,000 – 100,000 years ago)

Ancestors of modern humans (appeared 150,000 years ago)

First footsteps

Human-like creatures first appeared about four million years ago and similar creatures have evolved since then. So when did our true ancestors first walk the Earth? A mere 40,000 years ago.

The first graffiti

People in Africa painted buffalo and other animals in their caves. Was it to brighten the drab rock walls? No one knows ...

AMAZING MESOPOTAMIA

One of the world's first civilizations began in Mesopotamia, in parts of today's Iraq.

FIRST FARMERS

People had *gathered* crops for thousands of years, but now began to *plant* part of the harvest instead of eating it all. This guaranteed a supply of grain each year.

FIRST WRITING

Developed around 3500BC, cuneiform had *700* wedge-shaped symbols – imagine learning that alphabet!

ON WHEELS

Transport was easier once the wheel was invented 5,000 years ago. The first wheels were whole slices of tree trunk.

PYRAMIDS AND MUMMIES

Ancient Egyptians are known for their pyramids and the mummies placed inside them. When a pharaoh died, Egyptians went to great lengths to ensure his body and soul survived into the afterlife. Body organs were removed to storage jars, the body was padded with linen, spices, wine and salts, waterproofed and wrapped in bandages, then shut inside a painted, body-shaped coffin.

> It's all Greek to me

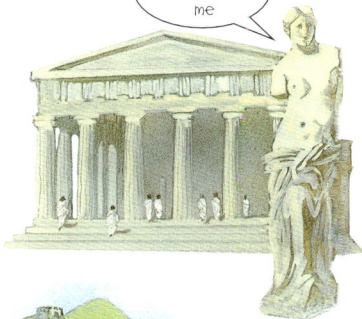

Raising Rome

Peasants settled near the Tiber River in Italy. This village would become the centre of the mighty Roman Empire.

Great Greece

Ancient Greeks were all-round achievers. Not just adventurous architects and talented sculptors, they made contributions to art, mathematics, philosophy, democracy and sports – the first Olympic Games were held in Greece in around 776 BC.

The Great Wall of China

China was a collection of small, warring states, all trying to pinch land from each other. The First Emperor of Qin unified these states. To protect his vast empire, he ordered individual defence walls be joined into one 6,000-km-long wall – fifteen thousand people died completing this task.

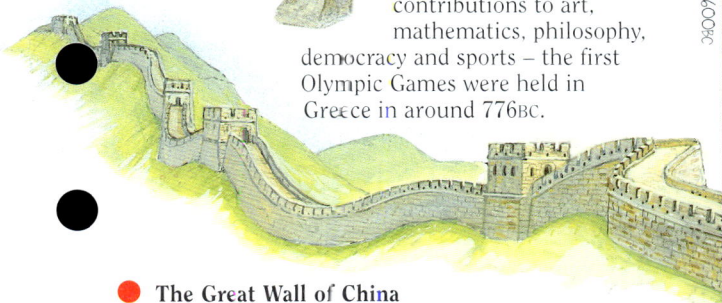

c3000BC

753BC

c600BC

221BC

3

The Roman Empire

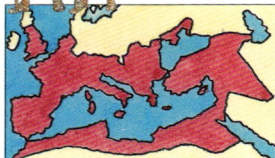

"Rome wasn't built in a day"

You've heard that phrase? Well it's true – the city of Rome grew from a tiny village into a huge empire, but it took *centuries*. In that time, Roman armies conquered the countries of the Mediterranean Sea and Europe. Roman soldiers protected the empire, marching along the straight roads they built.

TECHNOLOGY

The Romans built:
- bath houses
- paved streets
- amphitheatres
- drains
- fresh water supplies
- central heating
- long, straight roads

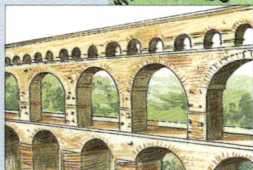

The Pont du Gard in France is a Roman-built aqueduct.

Latin for all

The Roman language, Latin, spread through the Empire and became the basis of many modern languages.

Pack your trunk

Hannibal, from Carthage in Africa, was a life-long enemy of the Romans. He marched 34 elephants across the Alps to smash through Roman defences.

Hello and goodbye, Julius Caesar

As a brilliant commander, Julius Caesar seemed unstoppable, but a year after he was made head of the Empire, suspicious senators stabbed him to death!

Jesus Christ – born before his time?

BC means Before Christ. Unfortunately, the modern calendar was miscalculated – and Jesus was born in 4BC!

4

The great time divide
The time after Christ's birth is called AD *(Anno Domini)*.

Constantine the Great
Emperor Constantine moved the capital from Rome to the city of Byzantium – a more central location. The city was renamed Constantinople after him.

Church built by Constantine, the first Christian emperor.

The beginning of the end
The Romans were not the only warlike people in Europe. In AD378 the Goths won a major victory against a Roman army. The Vandals, Franks, Visigoths and Huns followed, plundering Roman towns. In 410 came the final insult as Rome itself was raided.

Attila the Hun
Attila was a fierce Mongolian warlord, who led his savage and relentless army of Huns across Europe and into ferocious battles. When they reached Rome, the emperor decided bribery was the only way, and promptly gave him a beautiful princess to marry! Fortunately for her, Attila died suddenly on his wedding night!

We're a load of Vandals!

Death of an empire
The last Roman Emperor, Romulus Augustulus, was overthrown by the Vandals, who finally destroyed Rome.

Religions and Invasions

The mighty Maya

c500

Powerful city states made up the Mayan Empire of Central America. The cities were partly run by priests, who demanded human sacrifices for the gods. This meant a lot of wars, as warriors went off to raid other cities, seizing prisoners to sacrifice.

Paddling for Polynesia

c400–500

Brave sailors packed up their families, animals and food, and set off into the unknown. Carried by Pacific currents and blown by the wind, they eventually landed on Hawaii and Easter Island.

Birth of Islam

c570

Mohammed was born in Mecca (in today's Saudi Arabia). He founded the religion of Islam after disagreeing with aspects of other beliefs. Followers of Islam are known as Muslims and Mohammed himself wrote the Muslim holy book – the Koran.

The Arab Empire, c750.

THE ARAB EMPIRE

Mohammed encouraged his followers to convert to Islam as much of the world as possible. By his death in 632, his faith had spread through parts of Asia and Europe. Since then, Islam has spread to many areas throughout the world.

Ah! Tang News...

The Tang Dynasty of China

The Tang Dynasty (family of rulers) began China's 'Golden Age' – when the country became powerful and wealthy after a period of instability.

The first newspaper was printed in China in 745.

618

Charlemagne and the surprise coronation

Charlemagne (French for Charles the Great) was a military leader who fought hard against the armies that attacked Christian Italy. The pope expressed his gratitude by inviting Charlemagne to stay for Christmas. He waited until Charlemagne was praying, then snuck up behind him and crowned him the first Emperor of the Holy Roman Empire!

800

VIKING RAIDERS

The Vikings were fierce warriors from Norway, Sweden and Denmark. When their farmland became scarce (as population grew) they built longships and travelled Europe's rivers and the North Atlantic Ocean, raiding and trading as they went, reaching Iceland in 870.

800–999

The fiercest Vikings were 'beserkers'

● Vikings were brilliant craftspeople. They carved a dragon or sea-serpent prow on longboats to scare the enemy.
● In 982, Viking chief, Eric the Red was accused of murder and forced to leave Iceland. He sailed farther west than any other Viking – all the way to Greenland.

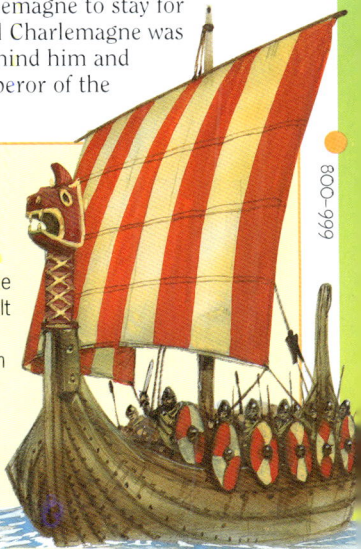

Discovery and War

1000
1003
1016-35
1050
1043-1099
c1050

New to New Zealand

In 900, the Polynesian seafarers had loaded their boats again and headed south. By 1000, Maoris (as these Polynesians became known) were established in New Zealand – as far south as Polynesians ever went.

Go back!

Oops, it's America

Leif the Lucky (son of the banished Viking chief, Erik the Red) became the first European ever to set foot in North America. He achieved this by accident though – his ships got lost on their way to Greenland!

Wise King Canute

Canute was a Viking king of England and Denmark. His grovelling courtiers declared him powerful enough to control the tides, which Canute knew he could not do. Wise Canute took them to the sea and proved them wrong.

BIG BANG IN CHINA

The Chinese invented gunpowder. At first it was used to make fireworks, but some spectacular weapons appeared later. This one fired arrows with a small gunpowder explosion!

Yoruba

In West Africa the Yoruba people formed a sophisticated culture which made intricate bronzes and terracotta pots. The largest states were Ife and Oyo.

Bronze head of an oba (king) of Ife.

Spanish hero

Brave but inconstant Rodrigo Diaz de Vivar (El Cid to his friends) fought both *for* and *against* Spain's Muslim invaders. But Spain still considers him a great hero.

Aahh!

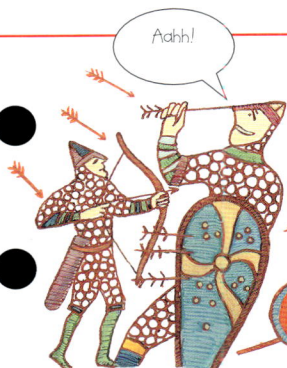

● **One in the eye for Harold!**
English king, Edward the Confessor, had promised his throne to William of Normandy, but was actually succeeded by his son, Harold. The enraged William invaded England to claim the crown – Harold was killed by an arrow in his eye!

THE CRUSADES

The Crusades were a series of holy wars between Christians and Muslims, mainly to claim Jerusalem – which is a holy city to both religions. Often as farcical as they were noble, the Crusades developed into many smaller battles between greedy knights eager to plunder and seize land.

Before the real crusades began, a rogue army captain, Walter the Penniless, and his friend, Peter the Hermit, led an unruly crowd of peasants across Europe slaughtering hundreds of people for no reason at all!

● First Crusade
1096–1099
Second Crusade
1147–1149
Third Crusade
1189–1192
Fourth Crusade
1202–1204
Children's Crusade
1212

Great Civilizations

The Chimus of Chan Chan

The Chimus lived along the coast of Peru and created a powerful state, called Chimor. They built a vast city called Chan Chan, grew their food in irrigated fields and caught fish along the coast.

Snap!

The Chinese invented picture playing cards, with hand-painted images.

Cheat!

SHOGUN SHOWDOWN

In Japan two powerful families quarrelled over who was to be the next emperor. In 1185 the Tairas were defeated by the Minamotos who set up a military government in the name of the emperor.

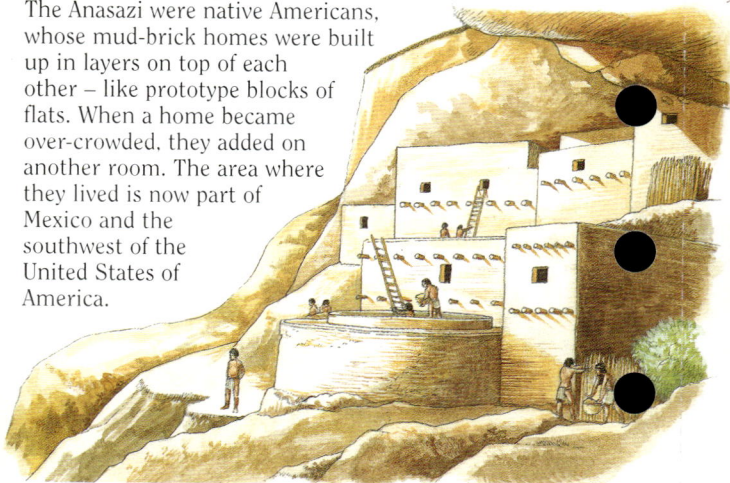

Room at the top

The Anasazi were native Americans, whose mud-brick homes were built up in layers on top of each other – like prototype blocks of flats. When a home became over-crowded, they added on another room. The area where they lived is now part of Mexico and the southwest of the United States of America.

Saladin the sultan

Salah-ed-Din Yusuf ibn-Ayyub (Saladin for short) was ruler and general of the Muslim forces in the Middle East. He united many Islamic peoples – and won back Jerusalem from the Christian Crusaders.

In 1192, the emperor gave Yoritimo Minamoto the title 'shogun' (which means great conquering supreme general). The Minamotos became one of the most powerful Samurai (warrior) families in Japan.

Tall tower totters

The Tower of Pisa was built, but with dodgy foundations it soon started to lean.

Mama mia!

Paper money appears

Fed up with carrying heavy copper coins, the Chinese introduced printed paper money.

Blow me down!

The first windmill with vertical sails appeared in Europe.

The Cahokia Mounds

The Cahokia people lived along the Mississippi River in south Illinois. They built huge, flat-topped mounds with temples on the top. The largest mound was called Monk's Mound, and was over 30 metres high!

The Toltecs of Tula

Between 900 and 1200 the nomadic tribe of the Toltecs, in Mexico, built the city of Tula with huge statues guarding from the temple roofs.

People who discovered these amazing statues thought they were aliens from outer space.

1138–93

c1150

1174

1180

c1200

900–1200

11

Warriors and Travellers

● Genghis Khan – the great chief

Genghis Khan was a Mongol warrior chief. With his army of 250,000 ferocious and merciless horsemen, he conquered most of Asia, slaughtering almost everyone in sight as he went. When he died, his empire stretched from China to Europe.

Genghis' empire was so huge that it took him almost a year to ride from one end to the other.

● The Children's Crusade

Thousands of European children decided to set out on a march to the Holy Land. It was a total disaster – many died on the journey and quite a few were caught and sold as slaves.

The Magna Carta

For the first time, people questioned a king's absolute right to govern. English barons ganged up on King John and made him sign a document, the Magna Carta, which stated rules that the king must obey.

KING JOHN

12

● The Mali Empire

The great warrior king, Sun Diata, founded a new kingdom in Mali, in West Africa. It was a sucessful trading empire for hundreds of years.

Mali grain stores designed to keep out rats and damp.

● Most travelled teenager in the world

At the age of 17, Marco Polo became the most travelled teenager in the world – he was away for 24 years! Marco passed through many countries en route to China. Here he spent 17 years as a court guest of Genghis Khan's grandson, Emperor Kublai Khan. He returned to Italy laden with fabulous jewels and stories of the Chinese Empire.

● Typhoon trap

Japan was saved from attack by Kublai Khan, when a huge typhoon swept 150,000 of his attacking troops to their deaths in the sea.

● Osman the Ottoman

Osman I began the Ottoman dynasty (family of rulers) which ruled a great empire for 600 years. It was to stretch from Turkey to Egypt and parts of Europe.

● In focus

The first spectacles were invented in Italy.

War, Rebellion and Plague

EASTER ISLAND STATUES

● **The mystery of Easter Island**
All that remains of the Polynesian culture of Easter Island are around 600 of these giant stone statues. No one really knows what happened to the people that carved them, but it seems they spent so much time on the statues that they forgot to look after themselves!

● **The Tughluqs in India**
Ghiyas-ud-din-Tughluq founded a new dynasty in India. He was murdered by his greedy son, who arranged for a building to collapse on top of him.

Pity about the building!

THE HUNDRED YEARS WAR (116, REALLY)

This war began when Edward III of England claimed the throne of France and declared war on the French. The war continued off and on through the rein of at least four English and French monarchs.

● NEW LONGBOW SENSATION!
At the Battle of Crécy, England won a great victory using the newly designed longbow from Wales. Capable of slicing through an enemy's chain-mail from 200 metres away, longbows killed 10,000 French, with a loss of fewer than 200 English.

English and Welsh archers with longbows.

● The Black Death

In 1338 a terrible, deadly plague crossed Asia, spread to humans by the fleas on rats. By 1349 the rats had carried the plague to Europe where it killed millions more. The plague was nicknamed the 'Black Death' because before you died of it, your skin turned black.

THE PEASANTS ARE REVOLTING

● FRANCE

A band of angry peasants attacked and killed French noble families. Later, hundreds of peasants were slaughtered in revenge.

● CHINA

Hong Wu, a Chinese peasant, led a rebellion against the Mongols and founded the famous Ming Dynasty of China.

Down with the rich!

We're revolting

● ENGLAND

Wat Tyler led an army of overworked peasants against the 14-year-old King Richard II. Protesting against the poll tax, they murdered the Lord Treasurer and Archbishop of Canterbury. Wat Tyler was killed too.

● Travellers' tales

Chaucer, an English poet, wrote The Canterbury Tales. He was the first major poet to write in English instead of Latin.

Death, Discovery and Art

● **What a way to go**
Henry Bolingbroke used a novel method to become king. He had Richard II stabbed to death, then made himself Henry IV.

● **Death of Tamerlane the Great**
Tamerlane was a Mongol warlord who tried to rebuild the empire of Genghis Khan. His armies invaded and raided large parts of Central, Southern and Western Asia, but his empire broke up when he died on his way to China.

● **Saint Joan of Arc**
At the age of 16, Joan heard what she described as "saints' voices" telling her to fight the 100 Years War. She fought two successful battles against the English before she was captured and burnt as a witch. She did not die in vain – her courage inspired the French to win the war.

MACHU PICCHU

● **Incredible Incas**
In seemingly hostile land, the Incas built the amazing city of Machu Picchu. The steep Andes mountain-sides were shaped into terraces for crops and stone homes. No one knows why this city was suddenly abandoned, and until 1911 it was unknown to the world.

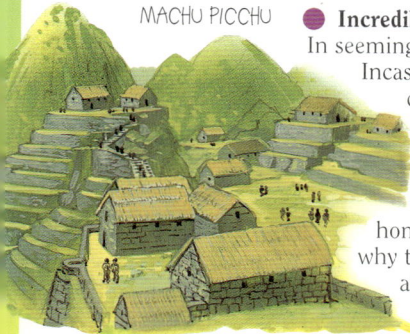

● **Inky fingers**
In about 1439, a German called Johannes Gutenberg invented movable type. Without his invention you wouldn't be reading this!

Europe re-born
The 1400s saw new enthusiasm for the arts, philosophy and learning. This was the Renaissance, (which means re-birth in French).

A star-gazer is born
Science could cause such scandal that Nicolaus Copernicus waited until he was close to death before publishing his theory that the Earth orbited the Sun. Seems obvious? Not when you consider that for 1,200 years before then, people had believed the Earth was centre of the Universe.

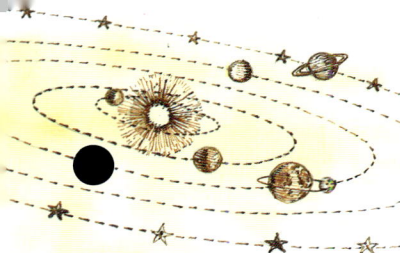

Leonardo
Leonardo da Vinci was a perfect example of Renaissance man! He was a great artist (he painted *The Mona Lisa*), an inventor (he drew plans for a helicopter), as well as an engineer, sculptor, scientist and philosopher.

NEW DISCOVERIES

DIAS SAILS SOUTH
Bartholomeu Dias became the first to sail around the Cape of Good Hope, Africa.

VASCO'S OFF TO INDIA
Vasco da Gama sailed round the Cape of Good Hope, and on – to find the first sea-route to India and its valuable spices.

THE EDGE OF THE EARTH
In 1492, people still thought the Earth was flat. Christopher Columbus set out to prove them wrong – by sailing from Spain to India going west not east. People thought he would fall off the edge of the world, but he made a great discovery instead – the Americas.

Emperors and Kings

● Michelangelo works flat out

The great painter and sculptor, Michelangelo Buonarroti lay on 30-metre-high scaffolding for 4½ years, painting beautiful images on the ceiling of the Sistine Chapel in Rome.

● Protestants' protest

Martin Luther, a German monk, nailed a list on a church door stating 95 protests against the way the Roman Catholic Church was being run. He and others formed a new type of Christianity called Protestantism.

● Henry VIII

Henry VIII was so desperate for a son to succeed him that when his first wife did not produce one, he divorced her and married again. Again no son appeared, so the second wife was duly dispatched ... Henry got through six wives altogether.

Catherine DIVORCED   Anne BEHEADED   Jane DIED   Henry   Anne DIVORCED   Catherine BEHEADED   Katherine SURVIVED

● Magellan sails away

Portuguese explorer Ferdinand Magellan led the first expedition to sail around the world. On the way he discovered and named the vital link – the Strait of Magellan, a passage of water leading from the Atlantic Ocean to the Pacific. Magellan was killed in a fight in the Philippines, but one of his expedition's five ships reached home after 3 years.

Byeee! See you around (the world)

● Ivan the Terrible

Ivan IV was crowned Tsar of Russia at the age of 17. He expanded his empire and ruled fairly, but then his wife died and Ivan went insane. He tortured, robbed and killed anyone he thought was plotting against him. He even killed his own child.

Really wicked!

● Suleiman the Magnificent

Suleiman I died after extending his Ottoman Empire to North Africa, western Asia and Mediterranean Europe. He had converted Christian Constantinople to Islamic Istanbul and built hospitals, mosques and bridges.

To be, or not to be...?

WILLIAM SHAKESPEARE

This famous English playwright, actor and poet wrote many sonnets (specially rhyming 14-line poems) and 38 plays in different genres.

• **Comedies** (A Midsummer Night's Dream; Much Ado About Nothing)

• **Tragedies** (Romeo and Juliet; Macbeth; King Lear; Hamlet)

• **Histories** (Julius Caesar; Henry V).

Shakespeare is thought of as the best-ever English writer because he was equally at home writing in any of these genres.

SHAKESPEARE'S GLOBE THEATRE

● Queen Elizabeth

Under Elizabeth's rule, England developed from an insignificant country into one that competently swatted aside the Armada that Philip of Spain sent in attack.

PLASTER CAST OF A DOG FROM POMPEII

● Lost city found!

Pompeii's story emerges. This city and its people were destroyed by ash, lava, mud and poisonous gas when nearby Mt Vesuvius erupted in AD79. The dead bodies rotted away, but their shapes became hollows in the ash and lava.

1530–84

1566

1564–1616

1588

1592

19

Colonies, Slaves and Civil War

● **Europe's cruel slave trade**
Europeans began to buy and sell
African people. Often they were
shipped to the Americas in harsh,
inhuman conditions, to work as
slaves in mines and plantations.

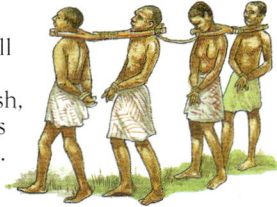

1600

● **Thirty Years War begins**
This war began when angry Protestant Christians tossed
the Catholic Imperial governors of Bohemia out of a
window to their death! Soon nearly every country in
Europe was battling it out.

1618

THE MAYFLOWER

AMERICAN COLONIES
● Fed up with the Church of England, a
group of Prostestants left England for
America, to set up a colony where
they could worship in peace. They
sailed through treacherous
storms in *The Mayflower*.

1620

● Dutch settlers founded
New Amsterdam (which later
became New York).

1626

*Hunting in
snowshoes.*

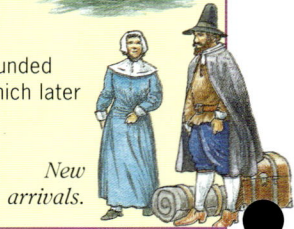

*New
arrivals.*

1628

● **The tomb of love**
When his much-loved wife,
Mumtaz Mahal died, the
Emperor of India,
Shah Jahan, built the
most beautiful tomb
in the world. The Taj
Mahal is carved from
white marble with
inlays of gold
and precious
gemstones.

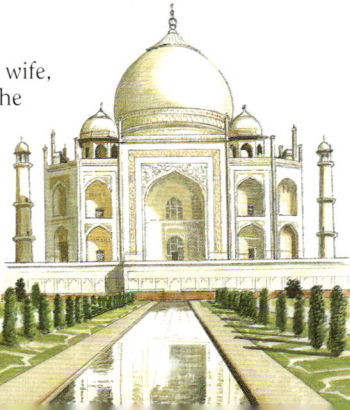

ROUNDHEADS v CAVALIERS

King Charles I of England ruled so appallingly that parliament gathered an army of its own and started the English Civil War. Parliament's army (the Roundheads) defeated the king's army (the Cavaliers) and in 1649 Charles I was beheaded. For the only 10 years in its history, England became a republic.

The nickname 'Roundheads' came from the shape of their helmets.

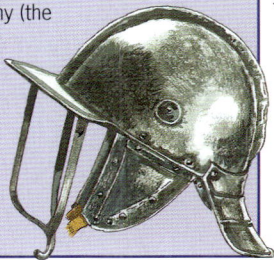

1642-49

● Manchus start dynasty

When discontented bandits seized Beijing, in China, the last Ming emperor committed suicide. A Manchurian general helped restore order, and decided his nephew, Shunzi should be emperor. And so began the Manchu dynasty.

1644

FIRE DESTROYS CITIES!

Fires wiped out the timber buildings of two of the world's major cities.
- THE FIRE OF EDO (later called Tokyo)
- GREAT FIRE OF LONDON
Nearly all of London was destroyed by a fire started at a baker's in Pudding Lane.

1657
1666

I spy with my little eye ...

● Telescopic sight

Isaac Newton invented the first mirror telescope, so astronomers got a clearer picture than ever before.

1668

Discovery and Revolution

PASTURES NEW

A series of inventions and discoveries led to a rapid change in farming.
- Jethro Tull invented the seed drill. It dug holes and then planted seeds in them – much quicker than by hand.
- Crop rotation methods improved – now each field could grow a crop every year.
- Animals were bred to produce more – for example, sheep were bred for wool *and* meat.

● Peter the Great – Tsar of Russia

Peter the Great was often harsh, but he turned around Russia's fortunes. As a young man, he travelled Europe in disguise, learning trades such as carpentry, boatbuilding, and gun-making. He took this knowledge and set about modernising his country.

I'm great!

To show that Russia was changing, Peter insisted the rich cut off their traditional beards. (They were only allowed to grow them back if they paid a special beard tax!)

● Rich pickings

When diamonds were found in an area of Brazil, hundreds deserted the sugar plantations to find treasure. The plantations almost closed down from lack of workers!

● Earth-shattering disaster!

Lisbon in Portugal suffers the biggest natural disaster of the century. An earthquake shook the city, killing or injuring fifty thousand and destroying two-thirds of the city.

● Cook explores the Pacific

Captain James Cook visits the Pacific Ocean three times, charting and exploring many islands, much of New Zealand, and Australia's coasts, for the first time.

The Boston Tea Party

The Amercian colonies began to resent British rule and the taxes they had to pay. To show that they would not be dictated to, a band of colonials boarded British ships in Boston harbour and emptied 300 boxes of tea-leaves into the water. This groundswell of opinion against Britain continued, and eventually led to the start of the war for independence.

Well, I declare

Declaration of Independence in the USA (4th July).

THE FRENCH REVOLUTION

The 'Storming of the Bastille' (the big prison in Paris) saw the start of the French Revolution. The ordinary people of France rebelled against unfair treatment from the French aristocracy – who had not bothered to call parliament for 175 years! The king, queen, and hundreds of French nobles did not realise the mass of bad feeling against them, and many were eventually executed by the guillotine.

Jenner's jab

Edward Jenner discovered a vaccination against smallpox, saving thousands of people from death each year.

This won't hurt a bit!

1773

1776

1789–1793

1796

A Time of Change

Army general, Napoleon Bonaparte, made himself Emperor of France. He launched successful military campaigns against many European countries (the Napoleonic Wars), leaving his family to rule the conquered countries. But in 1812 he invaded Russia. The Russians' tactics combined with the freezing winter reduced his 400,000 soldiers to just 30,000. He was finally defeated by Britain at the 1815 Battle of Waterloo.

1804

THE INDUSTRIAL REVOLUTION

Over the previous 200 years there had been slow but sure improvements in technology but the 1800s saw a sudden explosion in development. New machines were invented that made products quicker and cheaper to make, and factories were built to house them. People who had worked by hand at home now moved to towns to operate machinery. Canals, ships and railways were built to transport the products.

1812

1815

INVENTIONS

1829

• Gas street lights first used in London
• Davy lamp (first safety lamp for miners)
• George Stephenson's 'Rocket' (first steam train)
• Marconi pioneered wireless (radio) transmission

1896

DAVY LAMP

● NO to slavery

Slavery abolished throughout the British Empire.

● Zulu wars

The Zulus of South Africa were warriors of great stamina – they could charge for miles (on *foot*) and still fight. They waged war against the Boers (Dutch farmers) who were trekking inland from the coast. Initially the Zulus won the battles but at the Battle of Blood River they were finally defeated.

● Irish potato famine

At this time, the Irish people lived on potatoes and little else. When potato blight destroyed the crop, over a million people starved to death and millions of others left Ireland to start a new life in America.

● Workers unite!

The Russian thinker and writer, Karl Marx, wrote a book which laid down the foundations of Communism.

1848 – A YEAR OF REVOLUTION!

- The workers in France rebelled
- Revolution spread across Italy
- There was trouble in Austria, England and Ireland!

The Spreading Power

● **Rule Britannia!**
From 1850 onwards Britain, ruled by Queen Victoria, controlled more and more territory around the world. This became known as the British Empire and included the colonies of Canada, Australia and the whole of India. Britain became one of the most important industrial and economic powers in the world.

● **Gold rush down under**
In 1851, gold was discovered in Victoria, Australia. So many gold-diggers rushed to make their fortune that in 4 years Victoria's population rocketed from 77,000 to 333,000!

Strewth!

● **Monkey man**
In 1859, Charles Darwin published his book *On the Origin of the Species*. It caused a great sensation as in it he suggested that humans and apes had the same ancestors. In his studies and his books, Darwin laid down the foundations for the theory of evolution.

● **North against South in America**
The American Civil War began because of a dispute over slavery. The southern states wanted to keep their slaves, but the north, led by the president, Abraham Lincoln, believed all people should be free. Over 600,000 died in the war, until finally the north won.

● **Civil war ends**
Slavery is abolished in the USA.

Silly sale

In 1867, the Russians sold Alaska to America – although they later regretted it as oil was found there in 1960s.

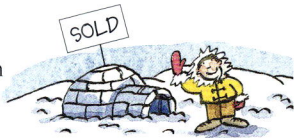

SOLD

A quicker way East

In 1869, the Suez Canal was opened between the Mediterranean Sea and the Red Sea. Ships could now sail a more direct route from Europe to Asia.

AMAZING INVENTIONS

- 1851 The first sewing machine
- 1853 Hypodermic syringe
- 1866 Dynamite invented by Alfred Nobel in Sweden
- 1874 The first pair of Levi jeans made
- 1885 The first sucessful petrol engine car made by Mercedes Benz
- 1886 Coca Cola was first sold
- 1892 The zip fastener was invented
- 1895 Marconi invented the first wireless.
- 1895 The first public film was shown in Paris.

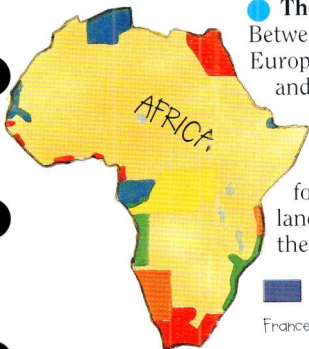

The race for Africa

Between 1870 and 1900 several European countries raced to claim and control parts of Africa to profit from the land's precious minerals and crops. The African people fought bravely to keep their land, but they were beaten by the guns of their enemies.

AFRICA

France   Britain   Germany   Portugal   Belgium

A first for women

New Zealand became the first country in the world to give women the right to vote in elections.

The World at War

1903

The first flight
Two American brothers, Orville and Wilbur Wright, made the first motor-powered air flight, over 35 metres in 59 seconds.

Henry's first Ford
The first mass-produced car, the Model T Ford, was built in the US in Henry Ford's factory.

1908

THE FIRST WORLD WAR

- The major powers of Europe went to war. The Allies (British Empire, France and Russia) fought Austria, Germany and the Ottoman Empire.
- Soldiers fought from trenches which stretched for 650 km along the 'Western Front'.
- German U-boats (submarines), British tanks and poison gas were all used for the first time.
- Around 10 million people killed.
- More than 20 million people wounded.

1914–1918

1917

The Russian Revolution
Discontented with the often tyrannical Tsars, and devastated by Tsar Nicholas II's poor planning in World War I, soldiers, workers and peasants revolted. Led by Vladimir Ilyich Lenin, power shifted away from the monarchy for ever.

● Killer flu

The worst-ever influenza pandemic (massive epidemic) swept across the globe, killing over 21 million people in just six months.

● Antibiotic accident

Scottish scientist, Alexander Fleming discovered the first-ever antibiotic – the mould, penicillin – when spores from it floated into some bacteria he was growing. The penicillin killed his bacteria.

● Coffee crisis

In 1927 and 1929 Brazil's coffee crops were so huge that the sheer quantity of coffee drove down prices worldwide. Impoverished coffee labourers lost out. This combined with a serious food shortage and led to a revolution in 1930.

THE SECOND WORLD WAR

- 1933 Adolf Hitler became leader of Germany.
- 1939 Germany attacked and occupied Poland, Belgium, Holland, Denmark, Norway and France.
  - 1941 Germany attacked and tried to invade Russia.
  - 1942 The United States joined in after Japan bombed the American fleet in Pearl Harbor.
    - 1945 Together, Britain, the United States and Russia defeated Germany.
      - 1945 The war against Japan was ended by dropping an atom bomb on Hiroshima.
        - Six million Jews and other peoples were killed in concentration camps.
          - A total of 50 million died during the war.

● Independent India

British India was split into two separate countries – India and Pakistan – and granted independence.

● Communist China

By 1949 China had become a Communist country, under the leadership of Chairman Mao Tse-tung.

1918
1928
1930
1939–1945
1947
1949

Peace and Technology

● **DNA discovered**
DNA (Deoxyribo-nucleic acid) is the chemical in the body responsible for what we look like and for making the body work properly. It was discovered by James Watson and Francis Crick.

● **King's dream**
Martin Luther King led the black people of America to demand equal rights by non-violent protest.

● **Europe united**
Six European countries formed the Common Market (EEC). More joined later – and it's still growing.

The Common Market.

SPACE RACE

The two main powers, Russia and the United States of America competed to be first in the discovery and control of space.
● 1961 The Russian, Yuri Gagarin, became the first human to orbit the Earth.
● 1969 The US astronaut, Neil Armstrong, was the first person to set foot on the moon.
● 1979 The probes, Voyager 1 and Voyager 2 reached Jupiter, then headed farther out.
● 1981 Space shuttles first launched.
● 1996 Hubble space telescope photographed distant galaxies.

SATURN 5
ROCKET

SPACE
SHUTTLE

● **Love and peace**
Many young people became 'hippies' and tried to find 'love and peace' through drugs, sex and rock groups such as the Beatles and the Rolling Stones.

Sisters unite!

● Death in Dallas
US President, John F Kennedy was assassinated by Lee Harvey Oswald.

● Burn your bra!
The Women's Liberation Movement began fighting for equal pay and work opportunities for all women.

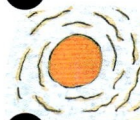

THE WORLD HOTS UP

Temperatures worldwide change as people destroy the environment.

- Rainforests cut down
- Air and sea polluted
- Acid rain
- The Greenhouse Effect
- Global warming
- Weather changes
- Floods worldwide
- Droughts

NELSON MANDELA

● Free Nelson Mandela
In 1990, Nelson Mandela, leader of the ANC (African National Congress), was freed after 27 years in prison in South Africa.

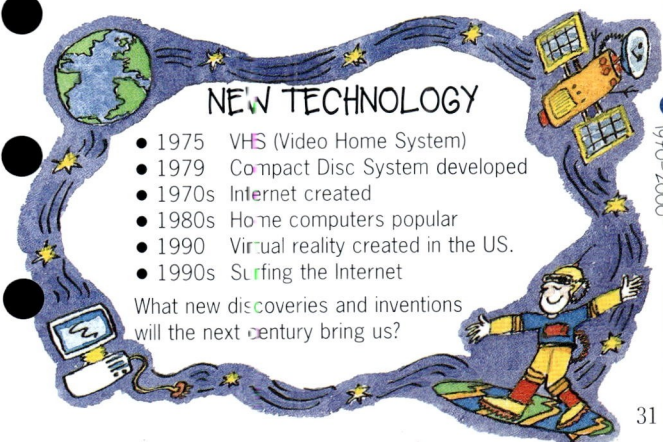

NEW TECHNOLOGY

- 1975   VHS (Video Home System)
- 1979   Compact Disc System developed
- 1970s   Internet created
- 1980s   Home computers popular
- 1990   Virtual reality created in the US.
- 1990s   Surfing the Internet

What new discoveries and inventions will the next century bring us?

1962

1966

1990s

1990

1970–2000

31

INDEX

Written by Carol Watson
Designed by Frances McKay

First published in 1996 by HarperCollins
Children's Books, A Division of
HarperCollins Publishers Ltd, 77–85
Fulham Palace Road, London W6 8JB
ISBN: 0 00 197933 7

Illustrations: Charlotte Hard,
Kevin Madison, Tony Smith

A CIP record for this book is available
from the British Library

Printed and bound in Hong Kong